Theo Fleury,
right winger.

MIND GAMES

Brett Favre,
quarterback.

Sammy Duvall,
water-skier.

M I N D   G A M E S

No Fear®: Explorations Into the Mental Arena of Sport
Copyright©1998 by Dr. James Beckett
All rights reserved under International and Pan-American Copyright Conventions.
Published by: Beckett Publications
15850 Dallas Parkway
Dallas, TX 75248
ISBN: 1-887432-53-1

Cover treatment, and all inside photos, by Tim Mantoani /
Tim Mantoani Photography (619) 543-9959
This book is authorized by the No Fear® company.
The staff of Beckett Publications would like to thank the good folks at
No Fear® for their time and complete cooperation.
All logos and sayings used with permission from No Fear® Clothing Co.,
2251 Faraday Ave., Carlsbad, CA 92008. (760) 931-9550.
No Fear® is a registered trademark of No Fear® Inc.
First Edition: October 1998
Beckett Corporate Sales and Information (972) 991-6657

BECKETT

ARE YOU AFRAID TO DIE, OR
JUST AFRAID TO LIVE?

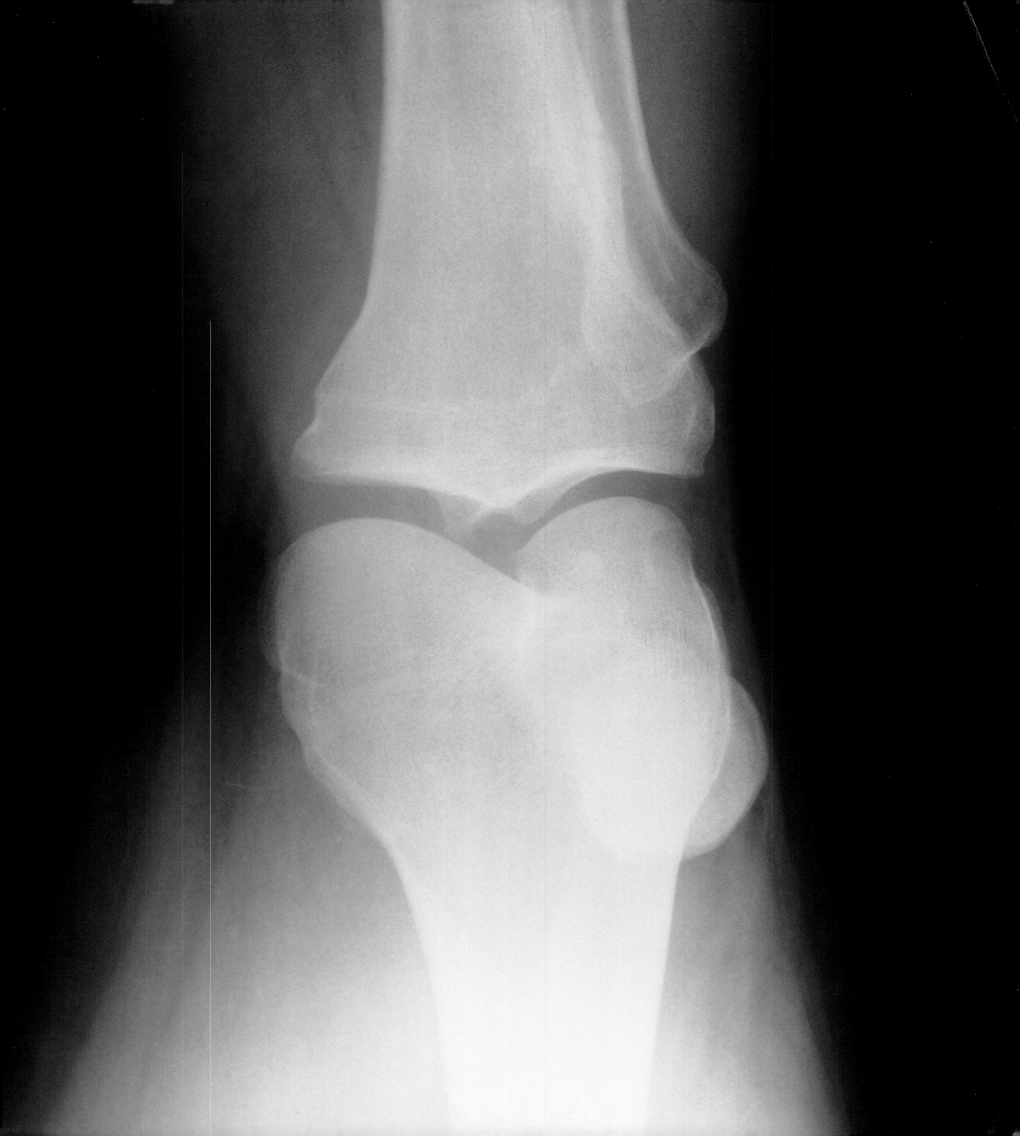

Greg Welsh,
triathlete.

F O R E W O R D

From that first moment when a child realizes it makes a difference if he wins or loses, his perceptions of life are changed. Child's play becomes competition, and as the child gains a measure of himself, he defines his dreams, hopes and aspirations. When the child's mind focuses on victory, he becomes a man.

The passion that grows in his heart brings much with it: commitment to hone his skills; an almost primeval desire to defeat any rival who walks on stage to face him; the will to endure setbacks, pain and adversity; and intense mental focus on the strategies and techniques of a chosen sport. The young man sets his sights on his dreams.

In the struggle to reach the very pinnacle of success — and who competes to finish second? — challenges arise, with consequences that can derail life. The most ruthless of Darwinian selection comes into play, crushing the weak and able alike, a never-ending process that separates wheat from chaff.

At every step, more and more of life's competitors realize the limitations of their abilities, their skills and their commitment. Each makes his peace and retires from the battle, his only solace being the knowledge that he pressed his limits, that he plumbed the depths of his soul.

With every new and higher level of refinement, the successful athlete's mental focus grows tighter — and more profound. The purest mental focus comes to the athlete once he has fulfilled all the other requisites of greatness: a nearly unconscious mastery of his craft and unyielding faith in his own physical ability. He can then operate on a different plane, and perform like someone from another planet. His body carries him where his mind wants to go.

Champions, those who have chosen to compete (and compete hard) in this game of life, are what this book is about. On the following pages, you'll find the greatest of champions in all sports, captured in brilliant full-color glory.

But even unquestioned champions — from Hercules to triathlete extraordinaire Greg Welsh — must understand that their greatness is but a shadow cast on the wall. So the champion athlete embraces each victory as if it were the first and last, and revels in it before the flood of time washes him away.

In the end, what separates the champion from the man who never dared is the memory of battles won and battles lost, and with that, the satisfaction of having measured his own soul.

M I N D   G A M E S

No Fear®: Explorations Into the Mental Arena of Sport

Mark McGwire,
first baseman.

ONE

DREAMS

DREAMS

"I want." It is part of our nature. As a species we learned long ago that some sense of worth comes from what is earned and what is lost.

So, as children we dreamed of conquests on school yard playgrounds. As adolescents, we dreamed of chicks and cars. Adulthood brings with it the quest for money and power, along with other things — the trophy, the cup, the belt — things that are not freely given.

They can only be acquired first by setting goals and then through victory. The prize is simply one thing taken from another. It is cherished and dreamed about because it's mine and not yours.

It is difficult to determine all that comes with it, as it is handed over from one champion to the next. What is really taken can't be seen. It is the erosion of another man's confidence, and the theft of his exhilaration for having won it in the first place.

It is the realization of our dreams. That is the sweetest taste of victory. But it should also be a reminder that the trophy is temporary.

It comes with one condition: It must be defended. It must be won or lost again. The appetite is never satisfied, and the dream continues.

Jesse James Leija, *boxer*.

Don't pursue your dreams, chase them down and tackle them.

Taylor Knox, *surfer. Always dreamed of being a surfer. Then he caught the largest wave at Todos Santos, Mexico, in 1997, earning himself $50,000.*

Mike Seipel, *barefoot water-skier. Mike invented the "inverted Seipel" when he accidentally inverted on a jump and flew 10 feet past the world record.*

It wouldn't be one man's dream if it wasn't another man's possession.

Sandy and Roberto Alomar, *Puerto Rican-born brothers. Both, like their father, followed their dreams to play in the Major Leagues.*

A dream is man's only true possession.

James Jett, *wide receiver and Olympic gold medalist, U.S. relay team. A tryout earned him a dream job in the NFL as a receiver for the Oakland Raiders. In his first season, he led the NFL in yards per reception.*

Marty Nothstein, *Olympic cyclist. The 1994 World Champion in the Match Sprint and Kierin was the first American in 82 years to win a gold medal in the Match and the first track cyclist in history to win gold medals in both events in the same year.*

Some people dream of success while others wake up and work hard at it.

Peyton Manning, *quarterback.*

Paralympic swimmer, *1996 summer games.*

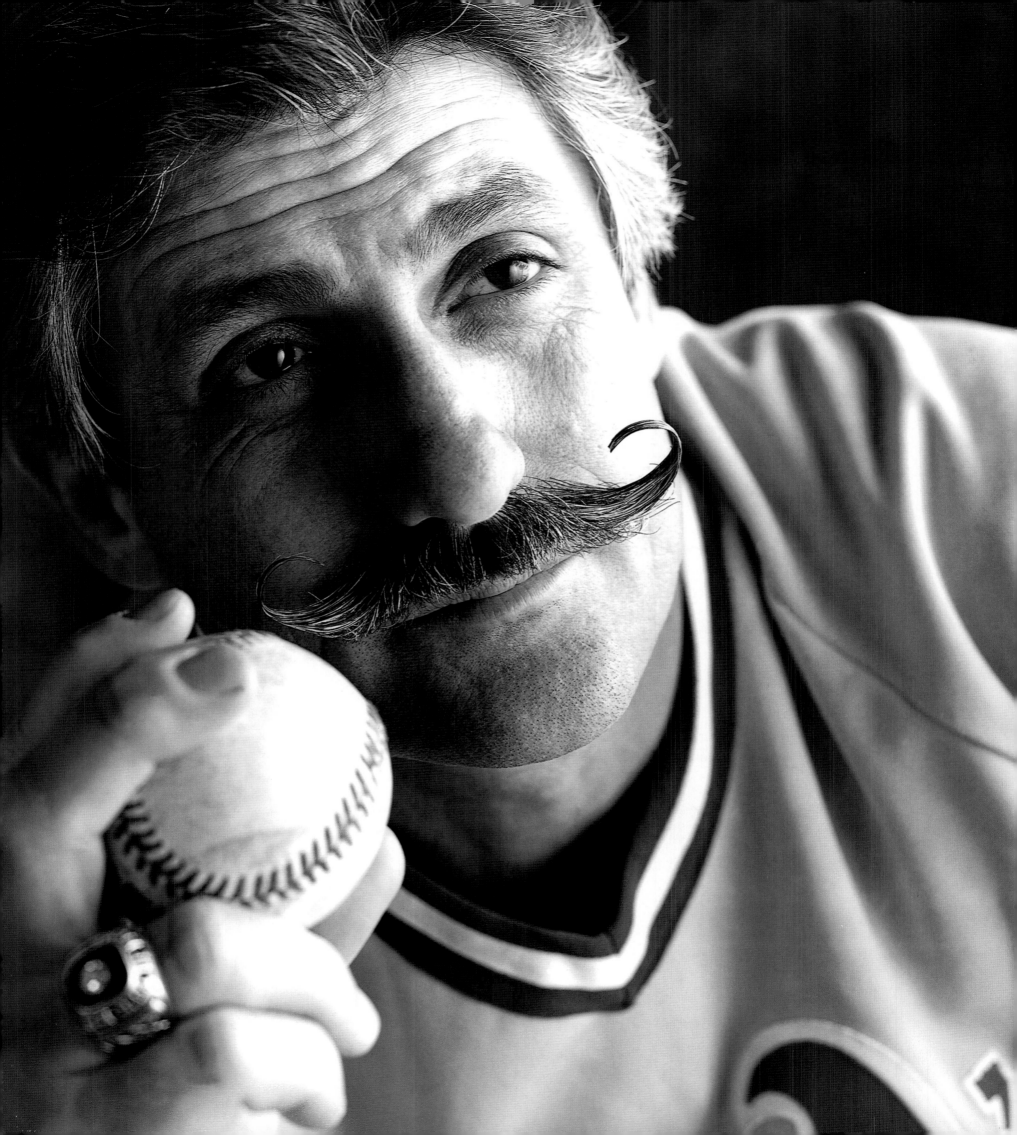

Fear: The thief of dreams.

Rollie Fingers, *Hall of Fame pitcher.*

Mike Piazza, *catcher. Not much of a prospect as a youngster,
Mike kept dreaming and collected 7 RBI in one game at
Philadelphia on Aug. 27, 1995. Exactly 1,389 players were taken in
the 1988 draft before Piazza. Just 43 players were taken after him.*

Beaten paths are for beaten men.

Graeme Cowin, *top-fuel drag racer, first Australian to break the quarter-mile record at 4.88 seconds.*

Michael Ronning, *downhill mountain biker.*

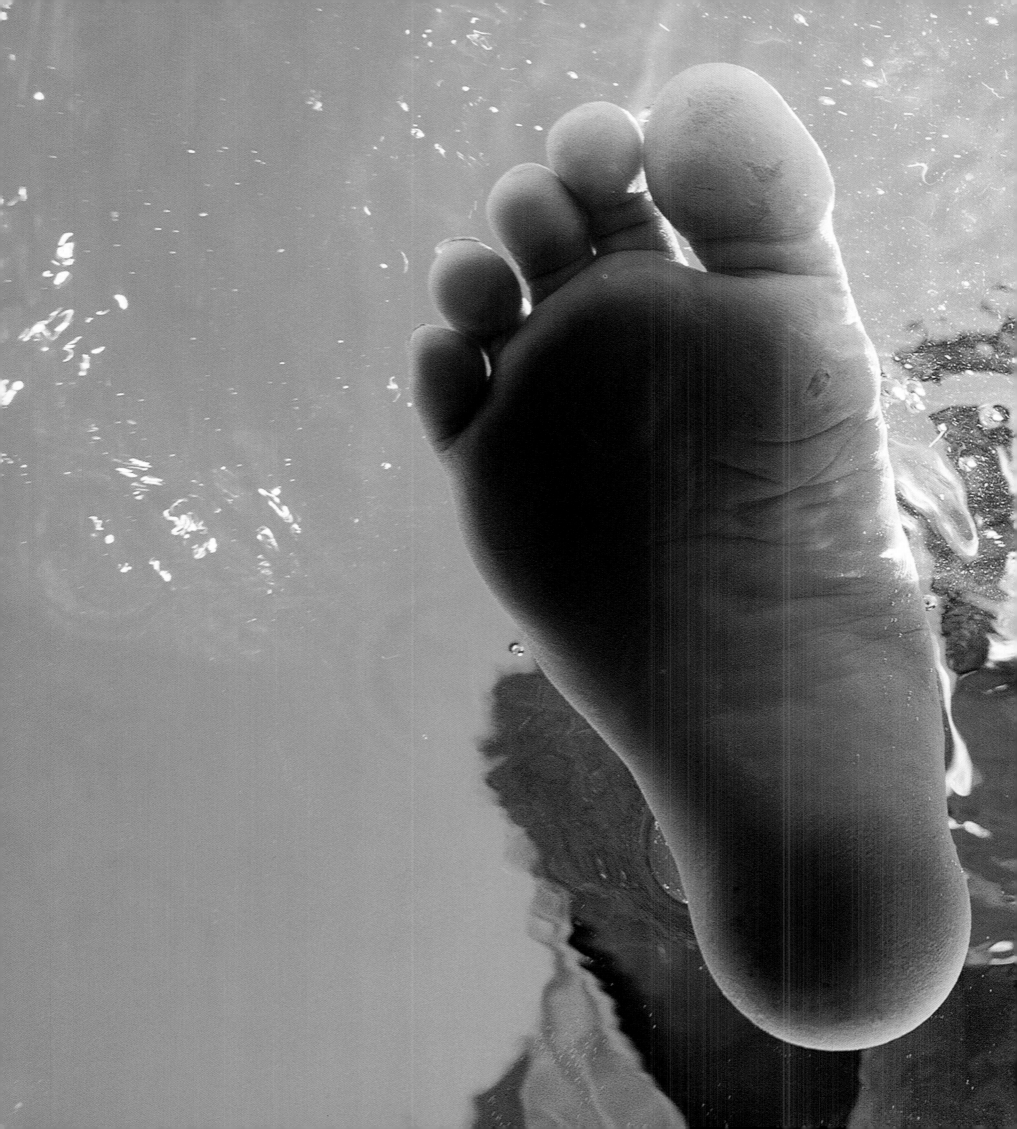

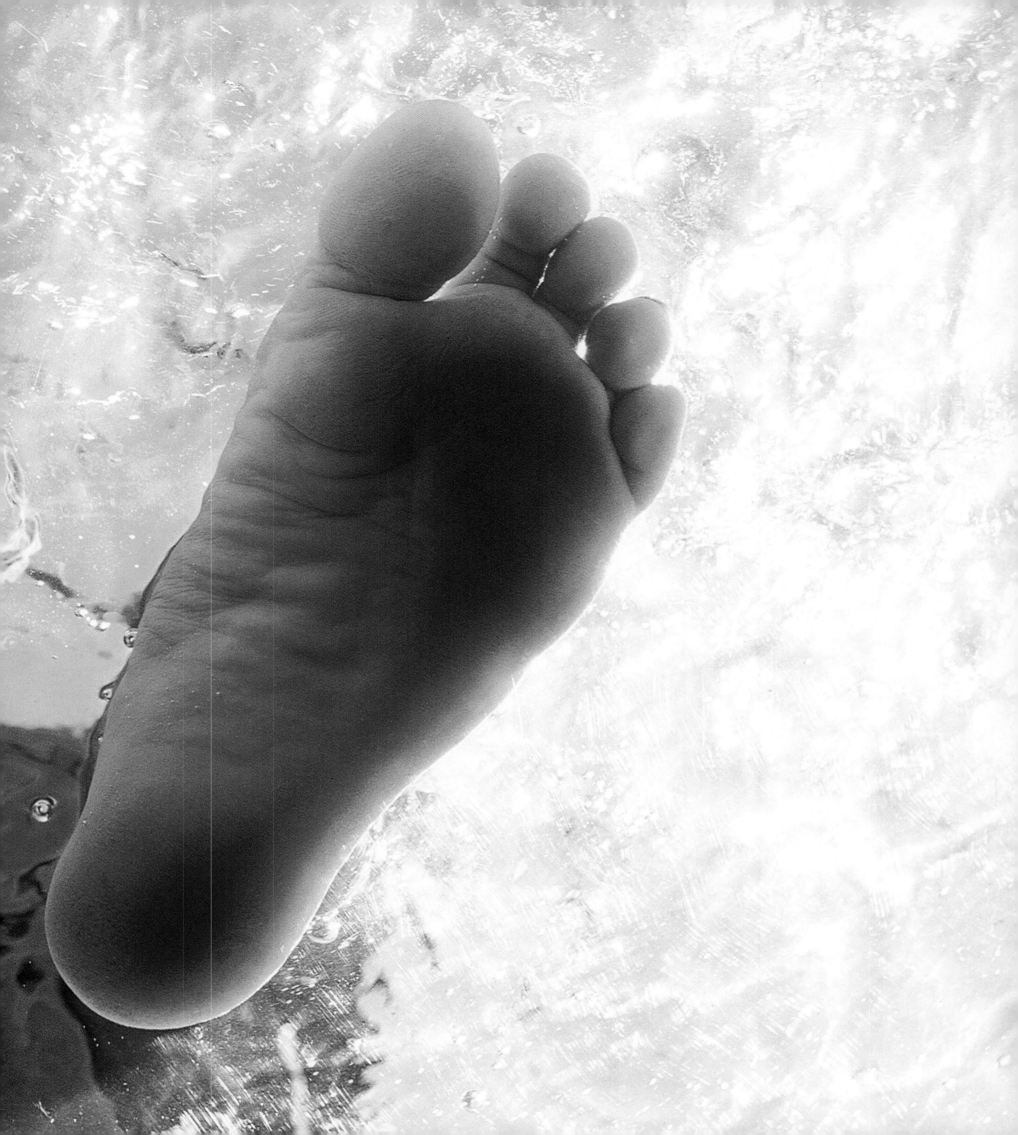

All men are great in their dreams, reality just narrows the competition.

Barry Sanders and his Heisman trophy. Barry, running back for the Detroit Lions, averaged 6.1 yards per carry in 1997 (he gained 2,053 yards that year). His ruggedness and determination allowed him to rush 40 times in a single game against the Cowboys.

Preceding pages:
Michael Ho, surfer.

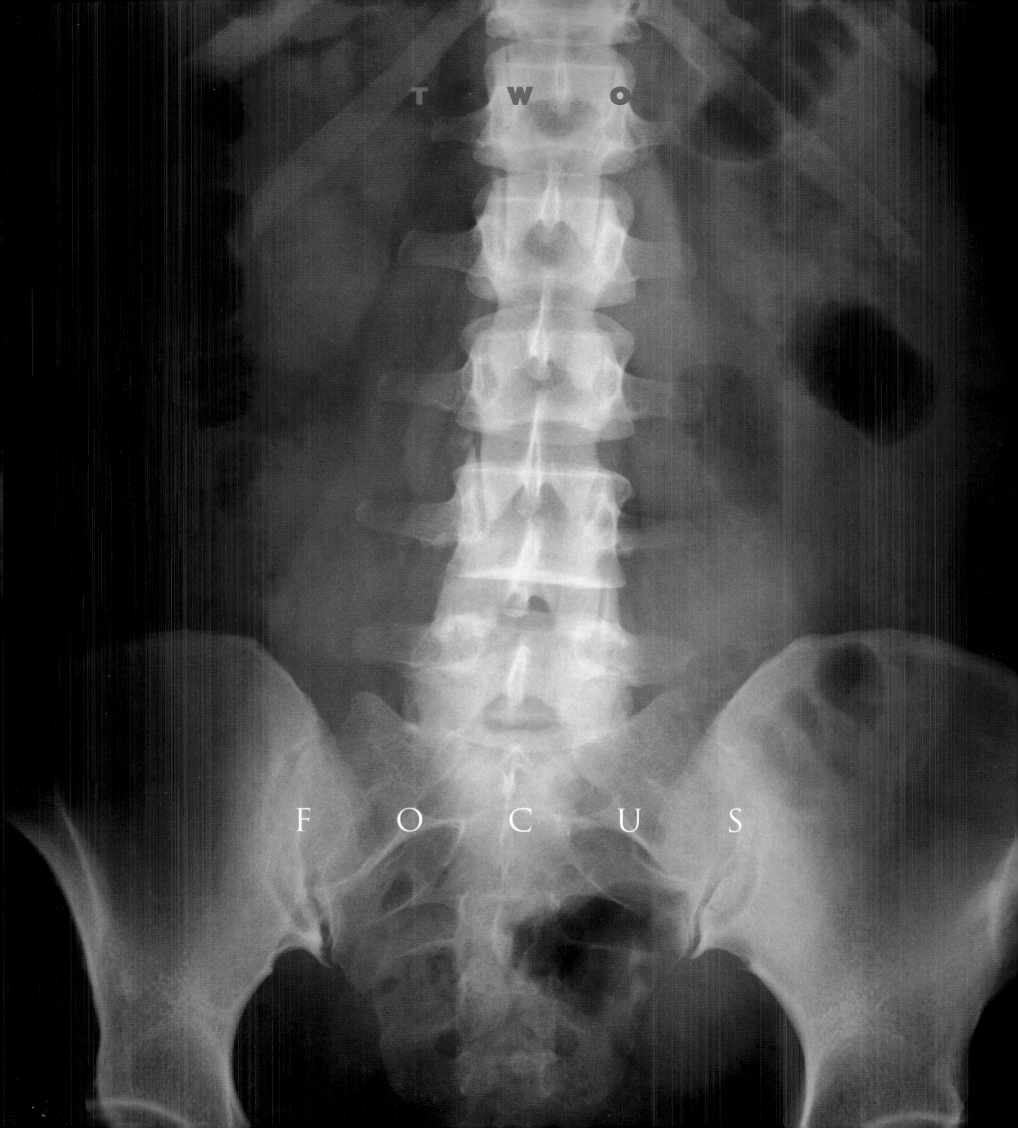

FOCUS

Many contemporary individual sports might confuse an ancient Olympian from Thebes or Athens. Though our sports test athleticism just as thoroughly as any Olympic event ever could, most incorporate elements beyond naked ability: the style of the surfer, the tools of a climber or the mechanical advantage of a cyclist.

In all such individual sports, a sense of style develops after the athlete has mastered his craft and then discovers he can find advantage over his rivals through personal expression.

Team sports however require a balance between the skills of the individual and the collective efforts of a team. The purest marriage of individual and team psychology is track and field's relay racing.

Four individual sprinters are linked into a team by a simple wooden baton they must pass between them, an act requiring focus and cooperation. The baton forces four supremely individualistic athletes to focus on the fact that they can only win if they win collectively. The individual cannot triumph over the group.

For the skilled athlete, focus on the end goal and everything in between can be fulfilled by the strength of mind and body.

Lorenzo White, *running back.*

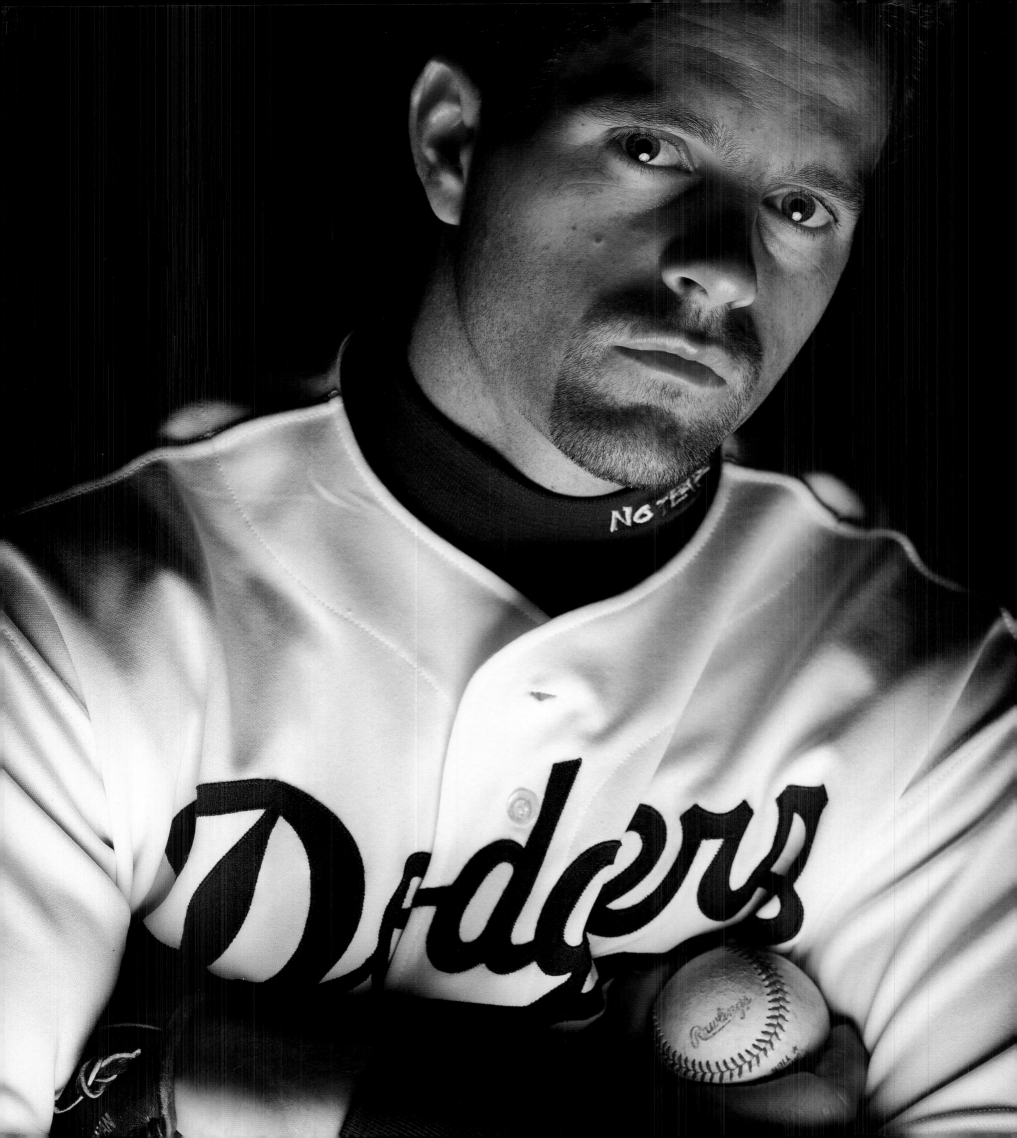

Competition can anger and discourage, but win or lose, it makes you better.

Eric Karros, *first baseman. Was focused enough in his first big-league season to win the National League Rookie of the Year award.*

Randy Ready, *utility baseball player.*

of strength, not a lack of knowledge, but rather a lack of will.

Jeremy McGrath, *racer.*

Jeremy McGrath, *six-time AMA national champion. Has more Supercross wins than any other rider in history.*

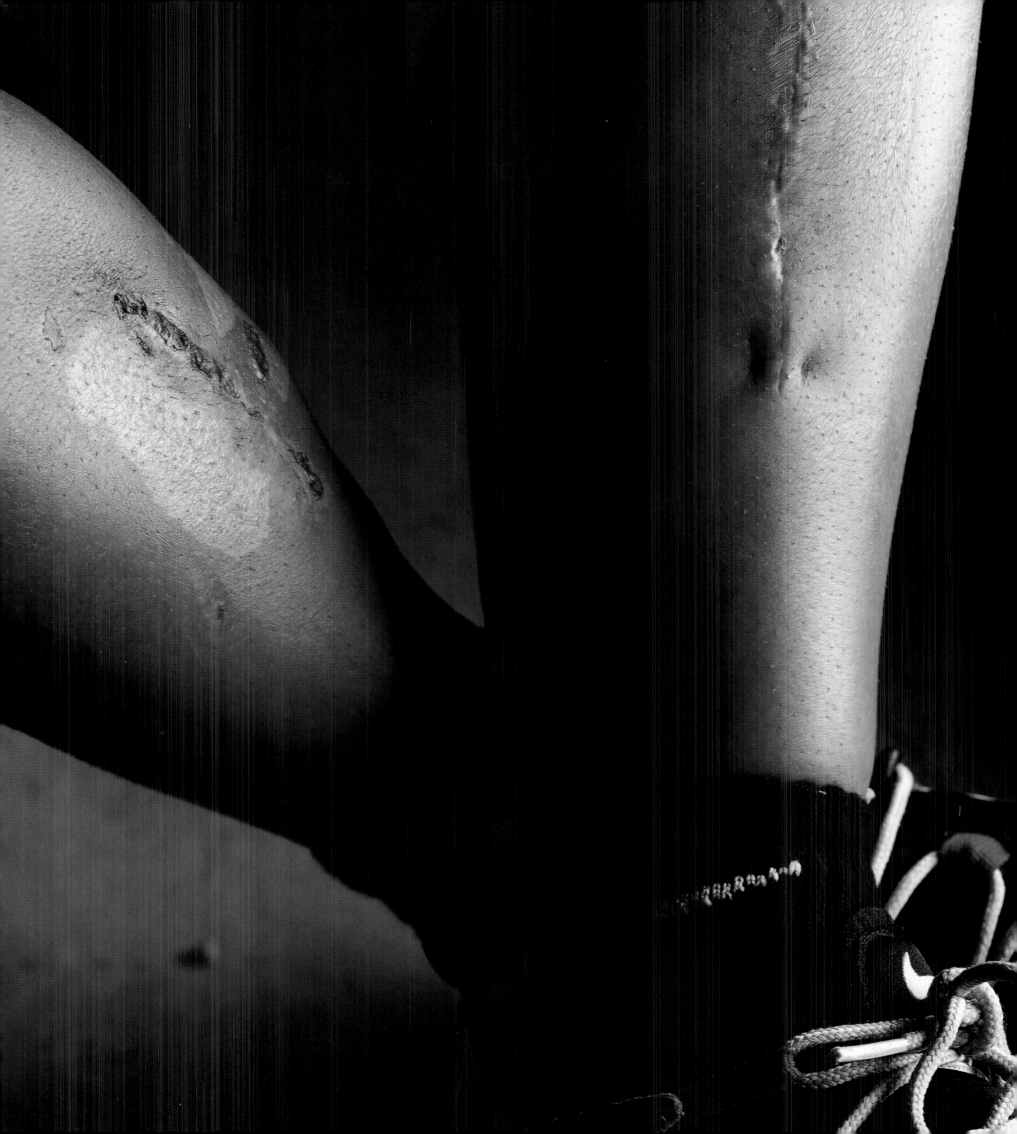

We take these risks, not to escape life, but to prevent life from escaping us.

Michael Joubert, *400 meter champion.*
Excess muscle build-up causing his calves to rub
together had to be surgically removed. Michael's
intense focus allowed him to work through the pain.

Luis Sharpe, *offensive lineman.*

Whatever the fear may be, look it in the eyes.

Ken Norton Jr., *linebacker, one of the most focused and feared defenders in the game.*

Wade Boggs, *third baseman, Golden Glove award winner in 1994 and 1995.*

Following pages:
John Randle, *defensive lineman, appeared in four straight Pro Bowls from 1993-96.*

Alex Rodriguez, *shortstop. Alex had no fear and entered the major leagues at age 18.*

Fear is born when desire dies.

Joe Juneau, *center.*

Darin "The SCUD" Shapiro, *has won almost every-thing in the sport of wakeboarding and continues to push the limits of what is humanly possible by going farther and higher every time he is on the water.*

Mark McGwire, *first baseman. Focused enough to keep his composure despite the annual hype surrounding the chase for 61 home runs. For the first time, batting practice became an event when Big Mac was at the plate.*

51

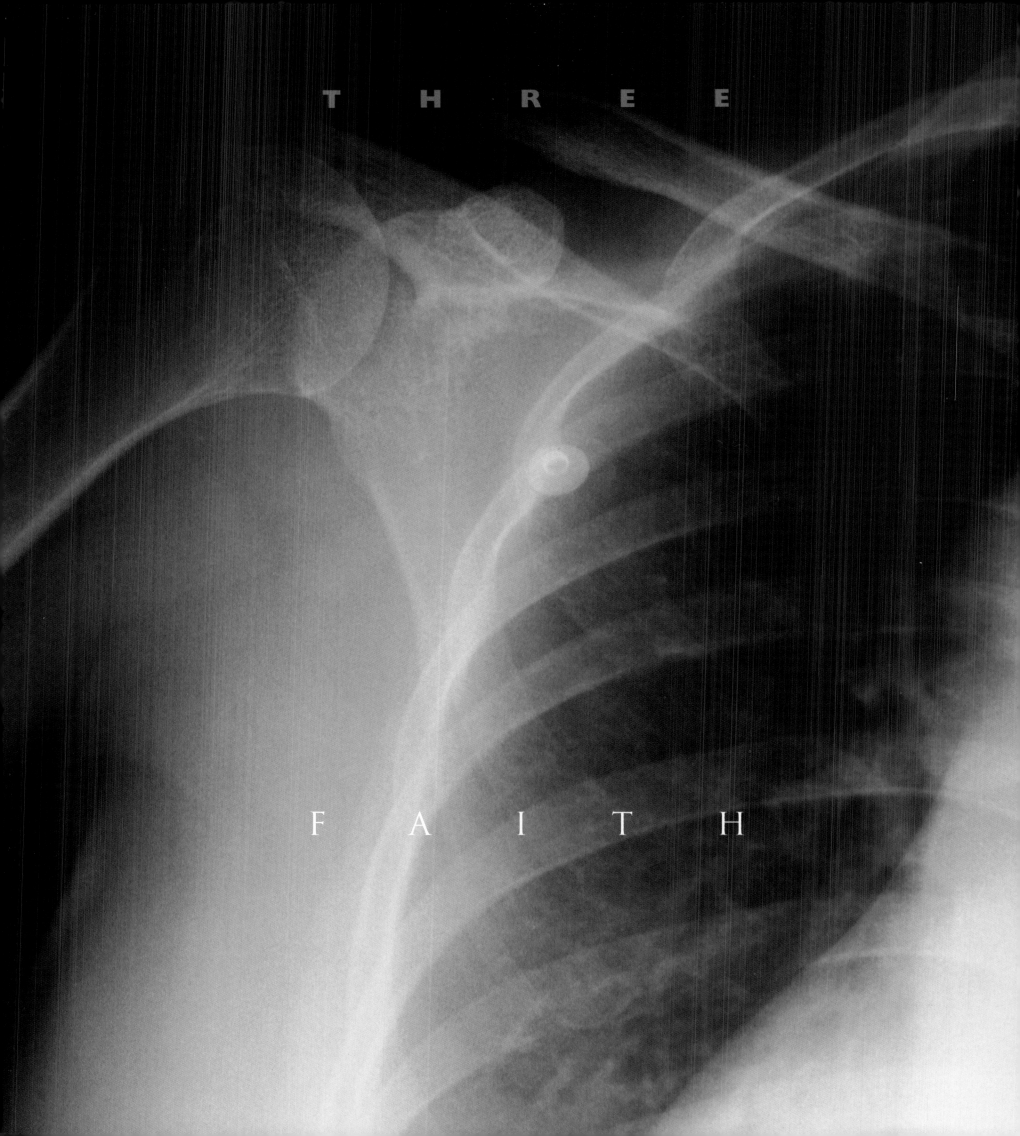

THREE

FAITH

FAITH

When you were young, you'd go to summer camp and you'd play that game where you would start to fall backwards with your eyes closed, knowing your fellow campers would catch you before you hit the ground. It's called faith.

But more important than trusting others is trusting yourself. If you don't believe you can do it, then you have already lost.

Oh, there will be adversity. There will be seemingly impossible odds. And you have to believe you can overcome them before you actually do it.

Some athletes will pray for guidance, looking to religion to help them find the way. Others look only within, hoping to find the strength it takes to do their very best. Hey, whatever works.

The important thing is to find that faith, and then never let it go. No matter what people say, no matter what they tell you you can't do, you gotta believe that you can do it.

No hill is too steep, no road too rough. Your inner drive demands that you try. It's in your soul to compete. You can't walk past that mountain without climbing it. Your destiny, my friend, calls for you to play.

Sammy Duvall, *world record holder, once jumped 220 feet, the equivalent of a 20-story building laid on end. His training includes two jumps per day.*

Sammy Duvall, *water ski jumper, in his backyard in Orlando, Fla.*

Kevin Kelley, *Featherweight world champion. Every punch proves it is not the size of the belt that matters, but instead the belief and determination.*

99 yards, 2 feet, 11 inches.
Are you going to knock on the door, or kick it down?

Jim Carey, *goalie.*

Jerome Bettis, *"The Bus," running back..*

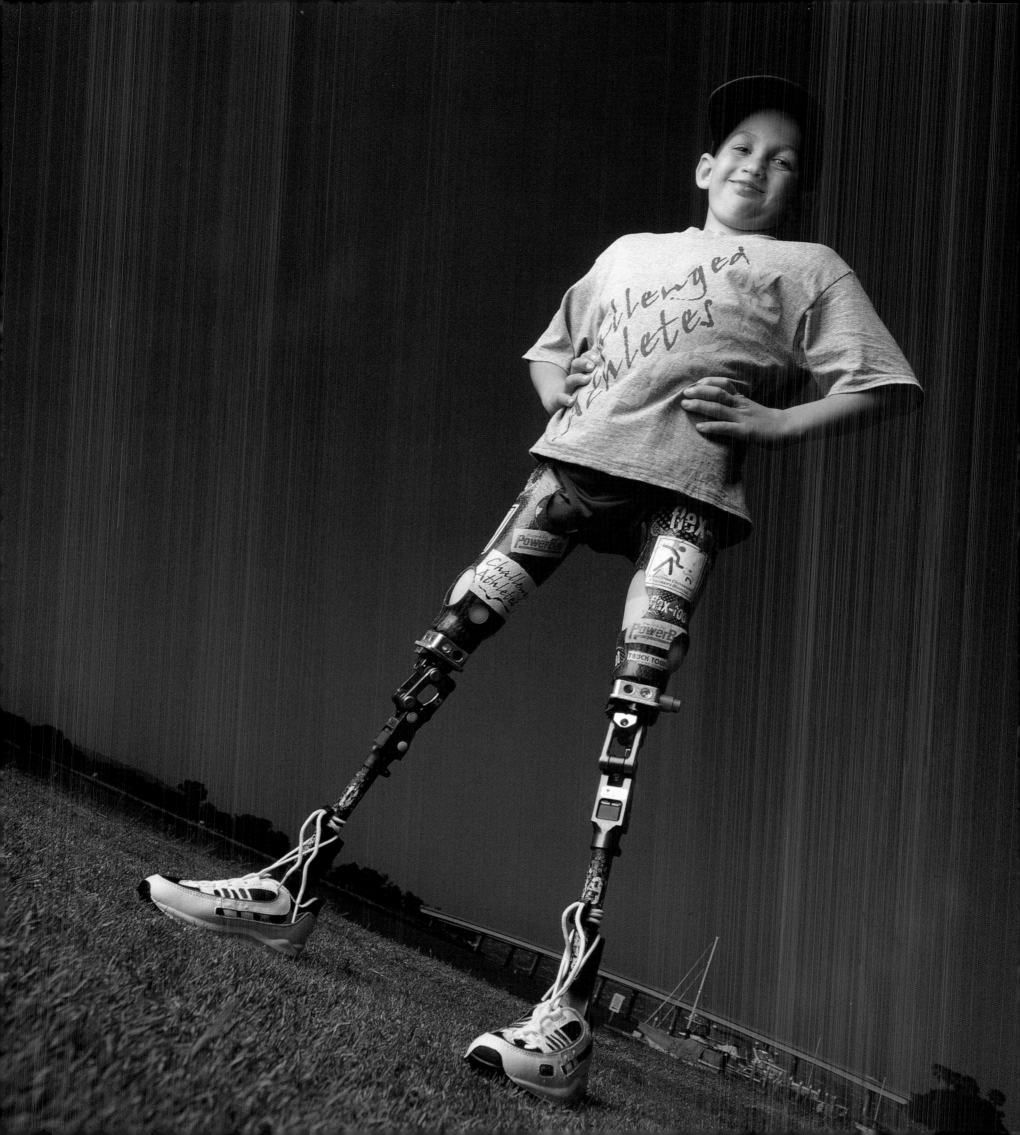

Rudy, *paralympic hopeful. Born with both legs joined together in a semi-fetal position, Rudy remained in a wheelchair until he turned 9. Told that he would only walk if his legs were removed, he gave the doctors the go-ahead for the amputation. His faith in himself helps him to compete in swimming and running events.*

Helmet of John Force burnt in cockpit fire.

SACRIFICE

Imagine not being able to go out in public without being mobbed. Imagine having to make special arrangements just to see a movie, or go to the mall. Still think being a sports superstar would be cool?

Everybody makes sacrifices. Professional superstar athletes sacrifice their privacy. Face it: They can't live a normal life.

All athletes sacrifice their bodies. There are certain things human muscles just aren't supposed to be able to do. After several grueling hours of swimming, biking and running, the muscles feel like they're on fire.

But the athlete continues, sacrificing short-term comfort for long-term gain. Football and baseball players can't afford to not dive for a ball just because they're playing on artificial turf. Heck, that carpet is as hard as concrete.

But still they dive, leaving bits and pieces of flesh in their wake. Think Ken Griffey Jr. is scared of a little turf? Think Jerry Rice has ever thought about the skin on his arms before lunging in the end zone for a catch?

Come to think of it, that hardcourt probably doesn't feel too good to guys like Dennis Rodman who will do anything to get the ball. It's called sacrificing the body. It's a part of the game. If you wanna play, you better get used to it.

Theo Fleury, *one of the smallest and toughest guys in the NHL. Not afraid to sacrifice the body.*

Albert Lewis, *cornerback*, knows the meaning of sacrifice. Although 14 NFL seasons have exacted a heavy toll on his body, Lewis is still considered among the league's premier pass defenders. Four straight Pro Bowls speaks for itself.

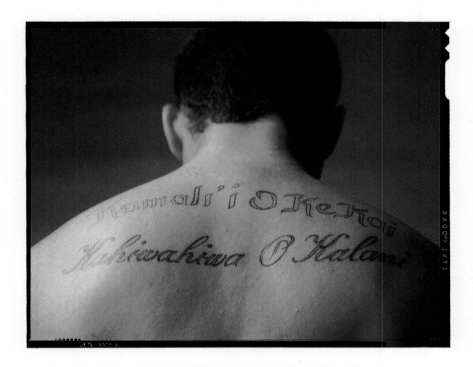

Sunny Garcia, *surfer. Known as one of the most powerful professional surfers in the world. Across his shoulders, it reads "Children of the Sea." Below that are the names of his children.*

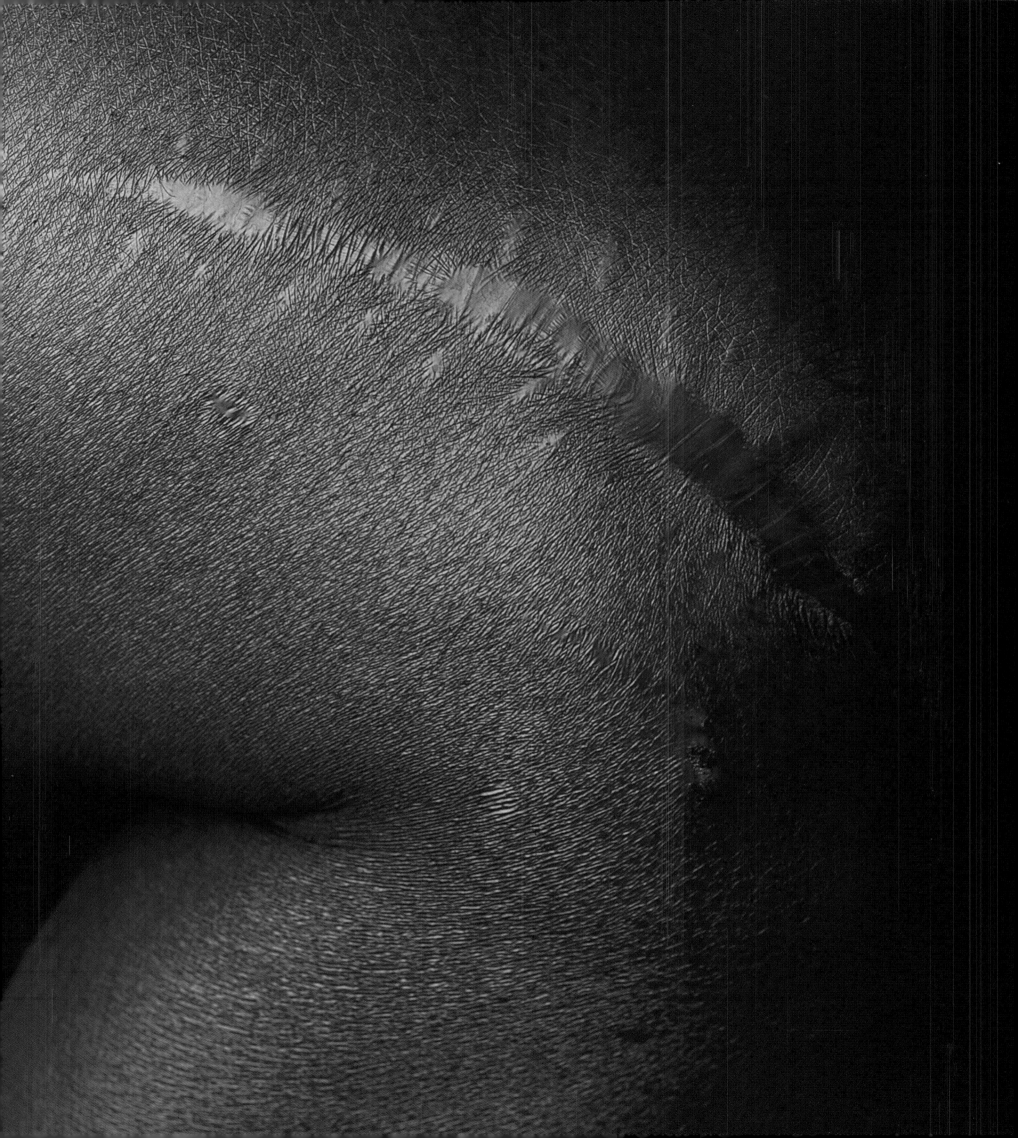

The road to victory is paved with flesh and bones.

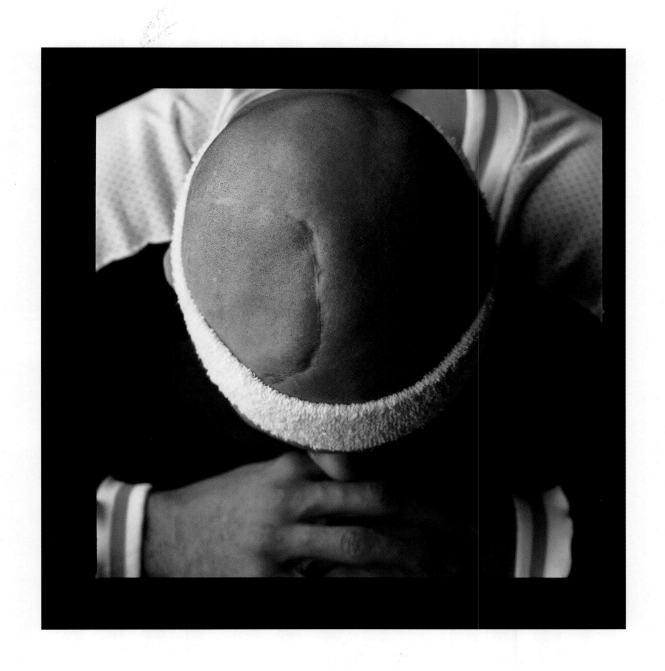

Derrick Walker, *tight end.*

Chris Gatling, *NBA All-Star.*

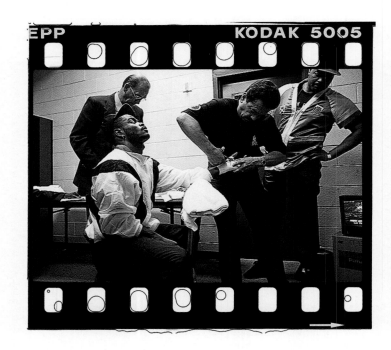

Terrible Terry Norris, *before a fight in which he regained his WBC title at the MGM Grand in Las Vegas. Norris has won the WBC super welterweight title three times. It took him five rounds to defend his title against Alex Rios and only 45 seconds to stop Joaquin Velasquez. He has successfully defended his title of the unified WBC/IBF 16 times.*

Terry Norris, boxer, Irish Spud Murphy's gym,
San Diego, Calif. Hundreds of hours of sacrifice in the
gym have led to a successful boxing career.

You don't need luck if you're good.

Aaron Slight, World Superbike Rider,
1991 Pan-Pacific Champion.

Mo Vaughn, first baseman, known for his power at the
plate. Vaughn is well respected in both the clubhouse
and the community.

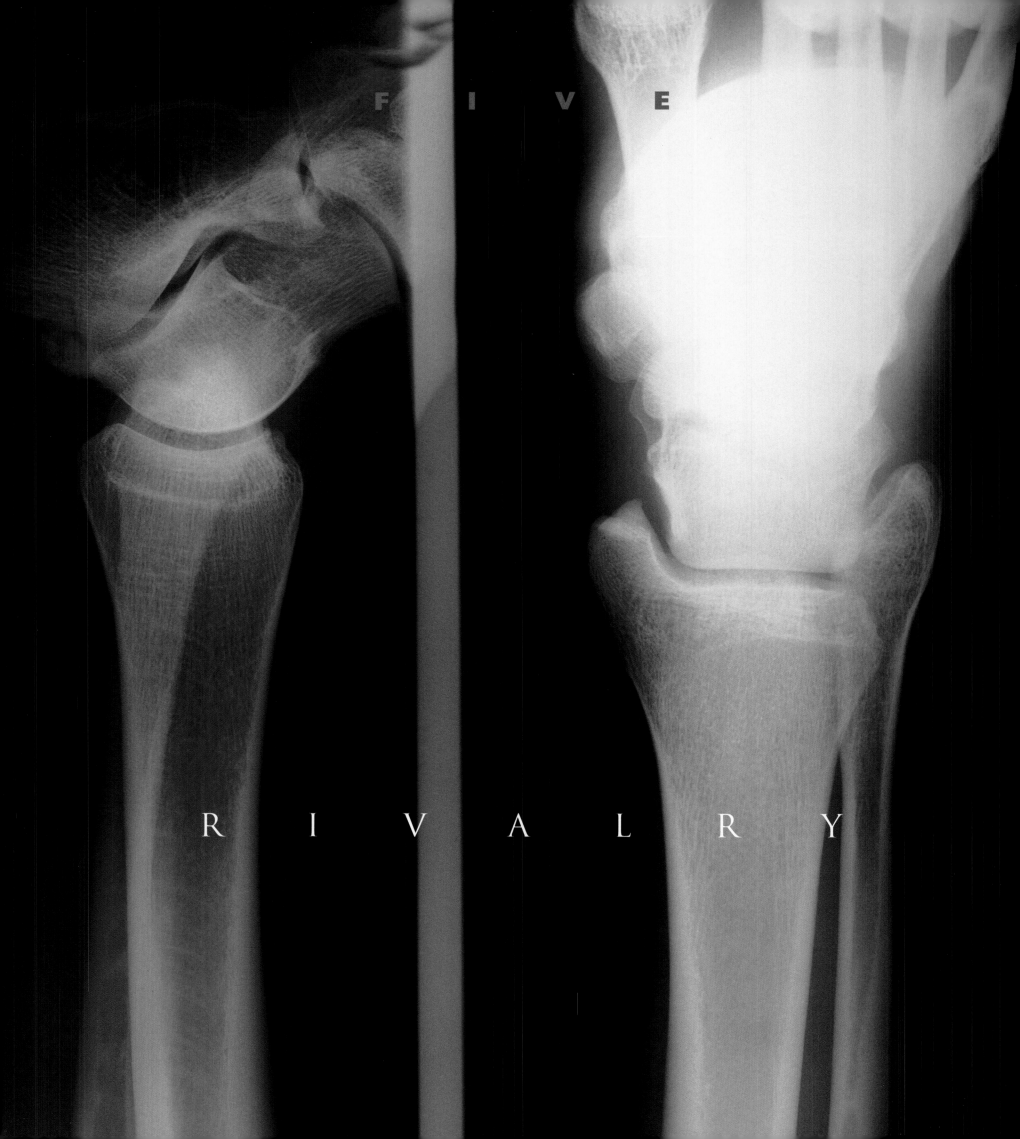

FIVE

RIVALRY

RIVALRY

Rivalry is the inescapable offshoot of our most basic human instinct: survival. From the act of conception, when millions of rival spermatozoa struggle against one another to fertilize a solitary egg and capture the prize of life, the human animal harnesses a primitive inner urge to battle opponents, outlast them, defeat them and win.

Some squander the miracle of life, avoiding competition, living in quiet desperation, measuring life in coffee spoons and might-have-beens. Others never lose the drive that first secured them life, and seek arenas crowded with worthy rivals.

Sports, politics, warfare, the natural world . . . all these arenas offer unrelenting rivals for the human animal prepared to compete.

Ultimately, man has only one rival greater than himself: time. All rivalry is a manifestation of our struggle against time and our desire to possess life.

Lose the will to compete, lose the desire to crowd one's time on Earth with as much life as possible, and death is but a faltering step away.

That's why those people compete. That's why they play the game to the best of their ability. And that's why they get more out of life than anyone else could ever imagine.

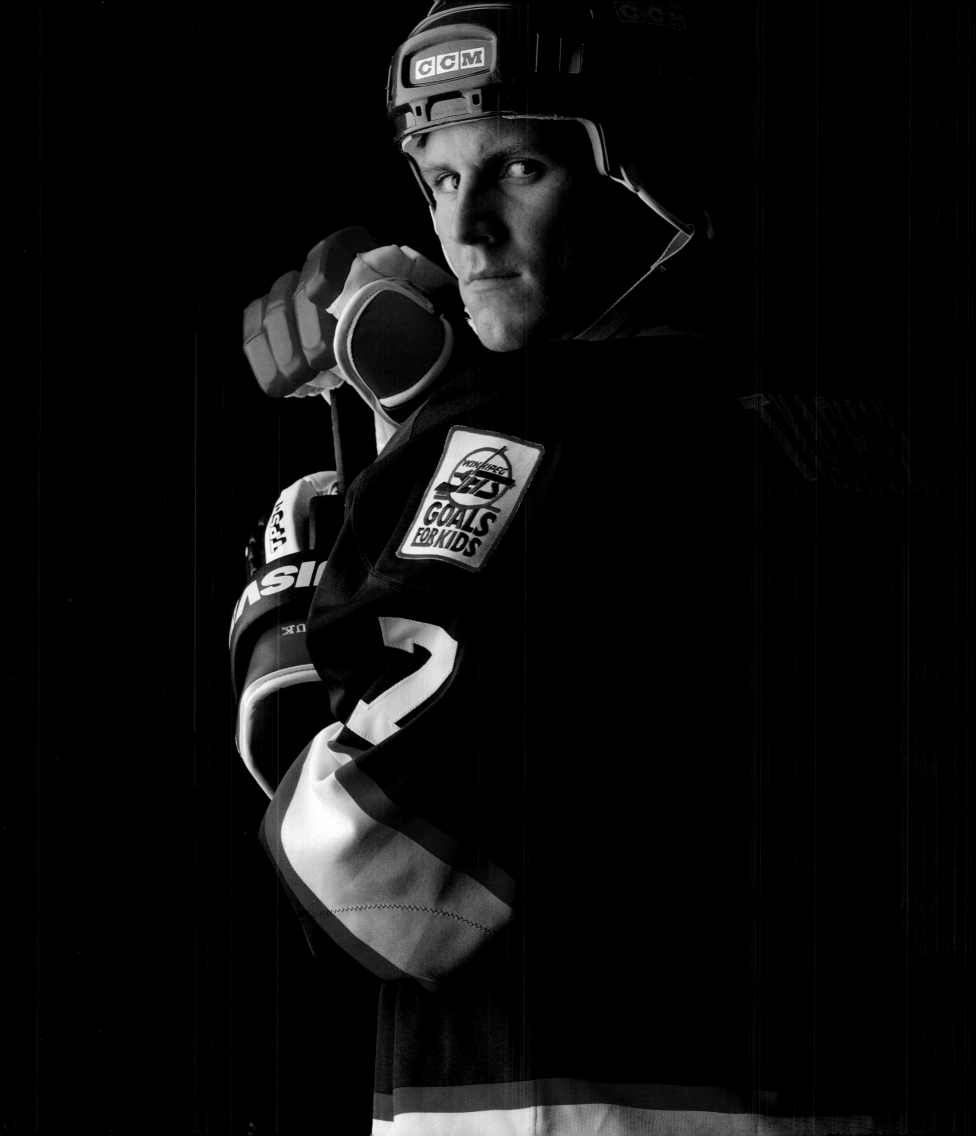

Keith Tkachuk, *left wing.*

Rivalry is more than just competition. It's personal.

Loy Vaught, forward.

Kobe Bryant, guard. Kobe outlasted his more
experienced rivals to win the Nestle Crunch Slam
Dunk competition his rookie season.

Man's greatest rival is himself.

Glen Plake, skier. Driven by a simple but hard-edged philosophy of life and a purist's ambition, he now exists in that rarified arena few athletes ever reach, where the battle is fought in the confines of his mind and soul to fulfill his own potential. Plake explores that inner rivalry while skiing on the snow-packed slopes of the world's most daunting mountains.

Dispose of your fear. Give it to your opponent.

Mark McGwire and stunt mannequin, *on the set of a No Fear TV commercial in which he is surrounded by pitchers who pelt him with baseballs.*

Rod Woodson, *cornerback, overcame the doctors' predictions after tearing his ACL in the first game of the 1995 season. His heroic rehabilitation efforts allowed him to become the first player in NFL history to suffer such an injury and return to play the same season.*

Muggsy Bogues, *smallest man in the NBA at 5-foot-3 inches.*

It's not that life's too short, it's just that you're dead for so long.

Leslie O'Neal, *defensive end.*

Julio Caesar Chavez, *boxing icon, training in Mexico City for an upcoming title bout. The bystanders are people from the city who wait daily for their national hero to appear. Chavez's training sessions are often open to the public.*

It's not about reaching goals. It's about rising above them.

Martin Bayless, *safety. Now retired, Martin coordinates several free football camps each year in which hundreds of aspiring youths come to learn from their NFL heroes.*

Greg Welsh, *1994 ironman triathlon champion. Greg develops his endurance with a grueling training regimen which annually averages 15,600 miles of biking, 3,120 miles of running and 224 miles of swimming.*

Jim Knaub, *wheelchair racer. Paralysis from a road accident ended his career as an Olympic pole vaulter, but his perseverance and indomitable spirit redirected his athleticism. Jim has three Los Angeles Marathon wheelchair wins, four Honolulu Marathon wheelchair wins and five Boston Marathon wheelchair wins (the vertical rise in the heartbreak hill section of this marathon is 400 feet). He brings his message of willpower to some 100 schools each year.*

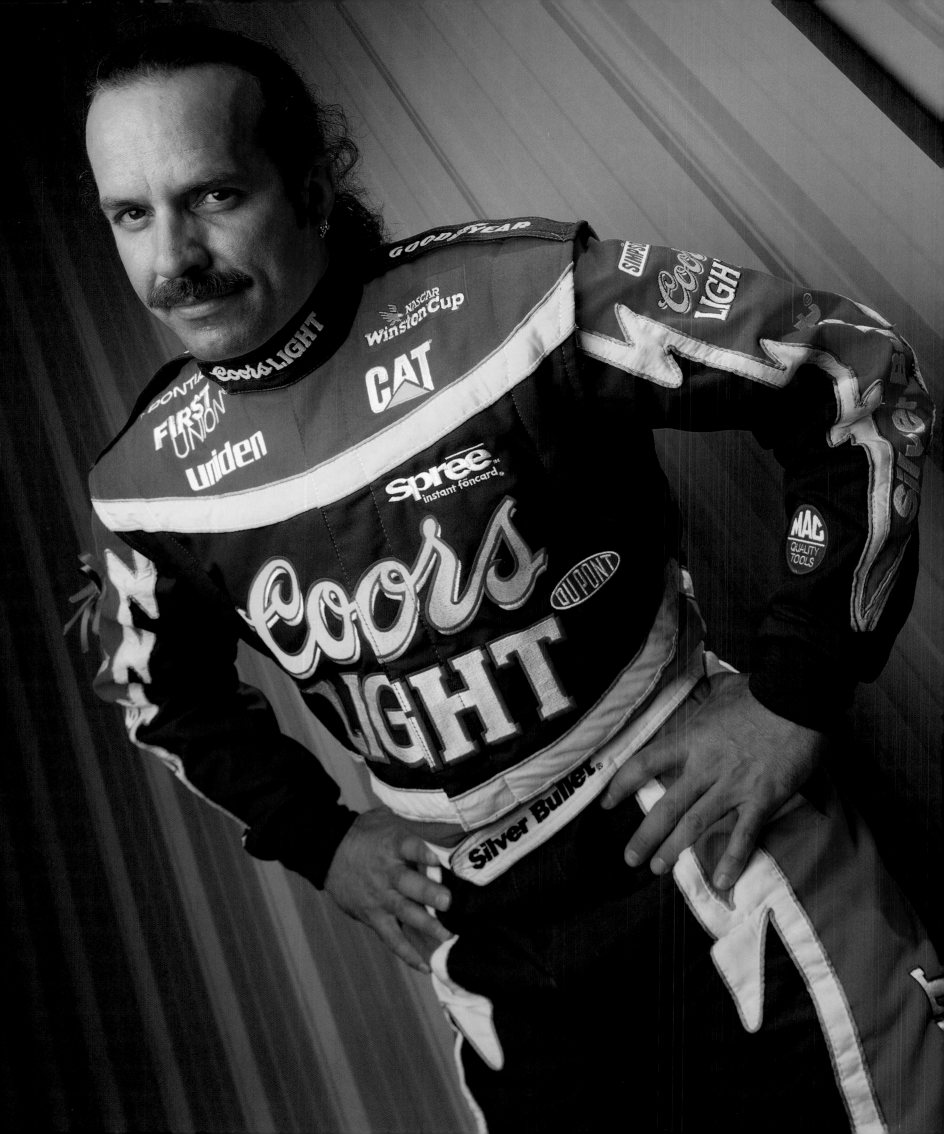

Absolutely, positively, most definitely, without a doubt, no fear (not even a little bit).

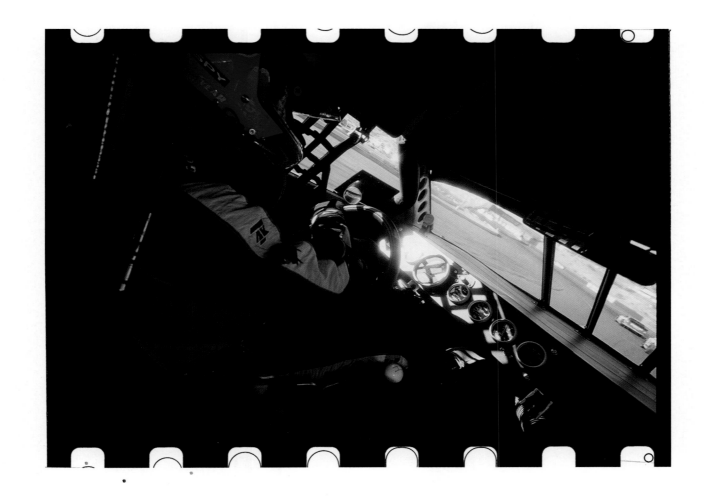

Kyle Petty, *NASCAR driver. Son of legendary driver Richard Petty and grandson of Winston Cup driver Lee Petty. Kyle's the first third-generation driver to win a Winston Cup race. Gramps won first in 1949, dad won first in '60.*

Kyle Petty, *turn 3 at Phoenix International raceway.*

Ernie Irvan, *NASCAR driver, survived a near-death crash in Michigan. Double-vision brought on by his injuries caused many to predict Ernie would never race again. His perseverance helped him defy the odds and he later returned to Michigan to take the checkered flag.*

Andres Galarraga, *first baseman, "El Gato."*

Teamwork is the fuel that allows common people to produce uncommon results.

Chris Calloway, *wide receiver.*

Donnell Woolford, *cornerback.*

Preceding pages:
John Timu, *Australian rugby player.*

Hans Rey, *trials rider.*

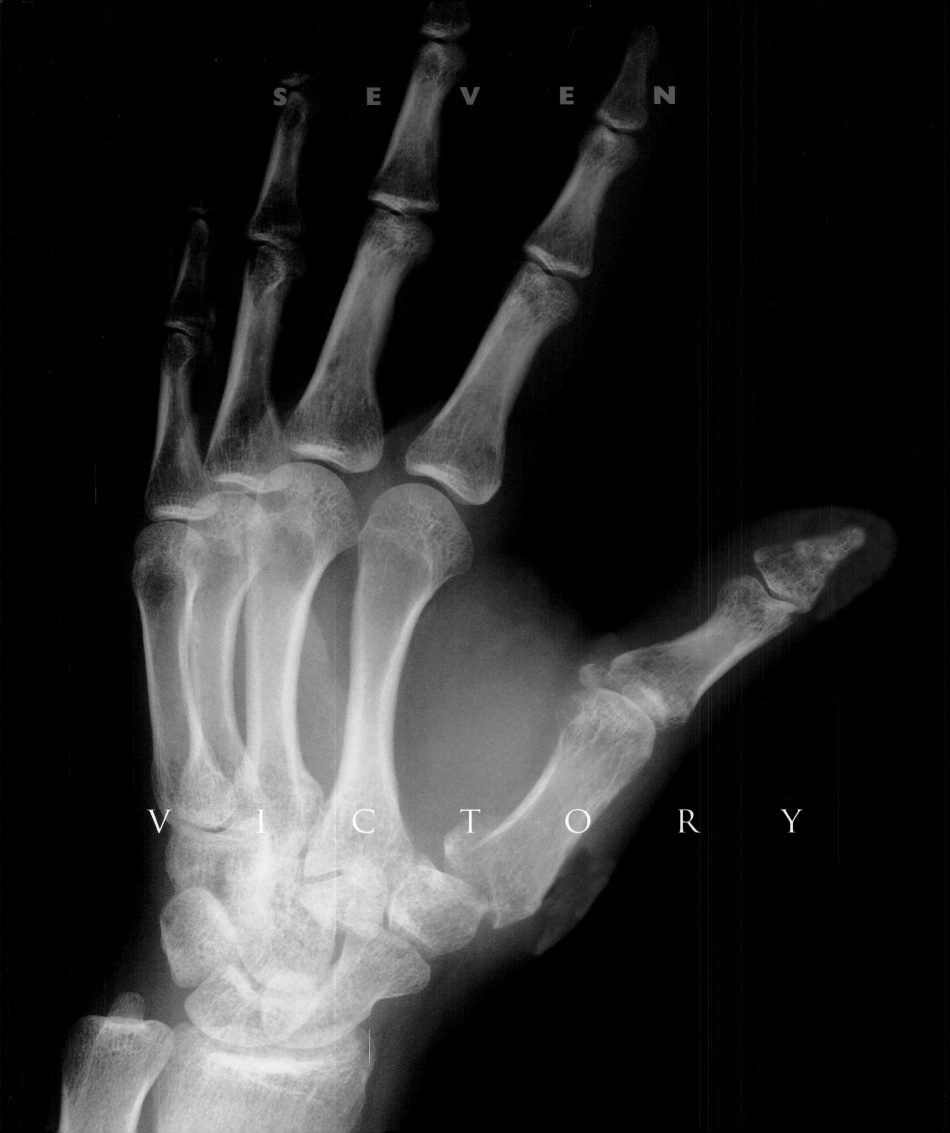

VICTORY

Victory. The whole idea is layered with meaning. You can just look at the scoreboard if you want. That certainly means a lot, but to say that's all that matters would be to dismiss everything else, all that you conquered to get there in the first place.

Along the way, there are sacrifices to be made, and a belief in yourself that must be developed. And there's fear, the one thing that can hold you back.

This may be the toughest obstacle to overcome, for it will eat your heart out if you let it. Fear — of whatever your opponent may be, the earth, the sea, the sky — will cost you more dearly and cause you more pain than any other person ever could.

It is through this realization, this intimacy and closeness with ourselves, that we see past the obvious battles with gravity, speed and the elements.

It is here that we discover one simple truth about competition: In sport, as in life, the real opponent, the only real enemy, is within.

Your primary opponent, your biggest rival, is your own fear. The battle can be won. It happens every day to people all around you. No need to be afraid. Go out and play.

Ty Murray, *six-time All-Around Cowboy titlist and unqualified all-around winner (consecutive titles from 1989-94).*

you've ever done . . . and one last chance to regret everything you never tried.

Ty Murray, Reno, Nev. In bull riding, 8 seconds
is considered a triumphant ride. Ty began riding his
mother's sewing machine case at age 2 (with spurs, of
course) and began competing at age 5.

Don't let your fears stand in the way of your dreams.

Ivan "Ironman" Stewart, *off-road racer. The sport's living legend with eight driver's championships.*

Tony "The Tiger" Clark, *first baseman, posing in a Hollywood studio with Rocky. By the end of the shoot, Rocky had the bat in splinters.*

133

Losers let it happen. Winners make it happen.

"Jesse" James Leija, *WBC world champion.*

Rick Johnson, *motocross Rookie of the Year and seven-time national champion. Retired from motocross and became Rookie of the Year in off-road stadium truck racing. A winner everywhere he's gone, he won the Baja 500 in 1995.*

GM
General Motors

Goodwrench

MOM 'N' POP'S

Snap-on.

FOOD CITY

GOODYEAR

AC

76

Goodwrench
wrench

Goodwrench
QUICK LUBE plus

Dale Earnhardt

NASCAR
Winston Cup

7 Time Champions

Where I come from, there is no next time,
there is no second chance, there is no time out.

Dale Earnhardt, *NASCAR driver.*

Michael Ho, *surfer.*

A champion is one who always gets up, even when he can't.

Terry Norris, *four-time WBC champion.*

Andre Waters, *defensive back.*

It's all fun and games until someone gets their eye poked out.
Then it's a sport.

John Purse, *BMX racer.*

Marty Cragghill, *superbike rider.*